CONTENTS

The Victorian Period
During the Victorian period there were many changes in politics and social life which shaped the way we live today. The photographs in this book are mostly of buildings and objects from that time.

The illustrations in this book are based on historical evidence. They have been painted by artists who have used drawings, photographs and descriptions from Victorian times to help them to decide how things would have looked then.

ROMAN BRITAIN 55BC to AD406	SAXONS AND VIKINGS 406 to 1066	MEDIEVAL BRITAIN 1066 to 1485	THE TUDORS 1485 to 1603	THE STUARTS 1603 to 1714	THE GEORGIANS 1714 to 1837	VICTORIAN BRITAIN 1837 to 1901	MODERN BRITAIN 1901 to the 1990s

ABOUT THIS BOOK
This book considers the Victorians chronologically, meaning that events are described in the order in which they happened, from 1837 to 1901. Some of the double-page articles deal with a particular part of Victorian history. Those that deal with aspects of everyday life, such as trade, houses and pastimes, are more general and cover the whole period. Unfamiliar words are explained in the glossary on page 46.

About the map
This shows the location of places mentioned in the text. Some are major cities, others towns or the sites of famous buildings or events.

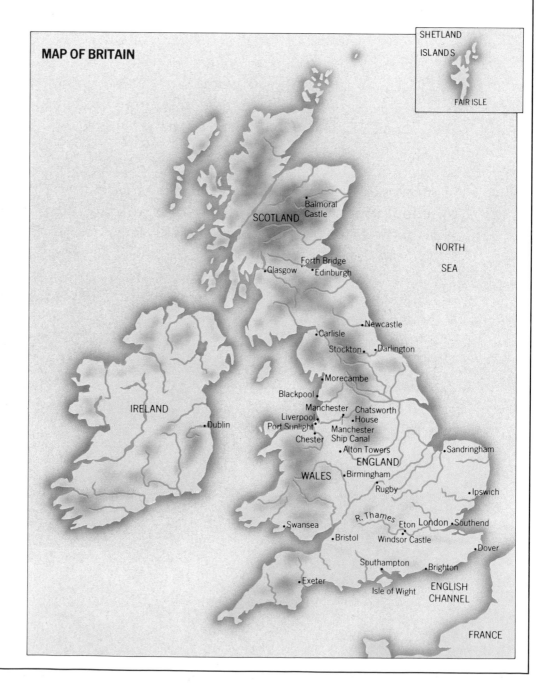

MAP OF BRITAIN

SHETLAND ISLANDS

FAIR ISLE

SCOTLAND

Balmoral Castle

NORTH SEA

Forth Bridge

Glasgow •Edinburgh

•Newcastle

•Carlisle

Stockton• •Darlington

•Morecambe

Blackpool•

Manchester Chatsworth
Liverpool• •House
Port Sunlight• Manchester
Chester• Ship Canal

IRELAND

•Dublin

•Alton Towers

ENGLAND •Sandringham

WALES •Birmingham

•Rugby

•Ipswich

R. Thames Eton London •Southend

•Swansea

•Bristol Windsor Castle

•Dover

Southampton •Brighton

•Exeter Isle of Wight ENGLISH CHANNEL

FRANCE

INTRODUCTION

Queen Victoria came to the throne in 1837. She reigned for over 63 years, until 1901 – longer than any other British monarch. During this time, Britain became the richest and most powerful nation in the world.

But the Victorian Age had a difficult beginning. The monarchy was very unpopular after the reigns of the wasteful George IV and the elderly William IV. There were violent riots by factory and farm workers, who wanted better wages and conditions. Some thought that Britain was close to revolution.

It was also an age of reform, or change. A series of Reform Acts gave thousands more people the right to vote for Members of Parliament in elections. Other new laws stopped young children from working in factories and mines, and made them attend school until the age of 13. Cleaner drinking water, sewers and better hospitals helped protect people from deadly diseases such as cholera and typhus.

The lands controlled by Britain grew into an empire which stretched from Canada in the west to New Zealand in the east. It covered nearly a fifth of the world's land area. Goods from the countries of the empire poured into Britain, to be sold on to other countries at a huge profit. More wealth came from industry. New machines, new factories and new methods turned out a huge variety of new products. People flocked from the countryside to find work in the rapidly growing factory towns. Steam trains made travel quicker and cheaper than ever.

THE YOUNG PRINCESS

"The Country is very desolate everywhere; there are coals about, and the grass is quite blasted and black … Everywhere, smoking and burning coal heaps, intermingled with wretched huts and carts and ragged children." Princess Victoria wrote this in her diary in August 1832, during a tour of the English Midlands.

Victoria was born on 24 May 1819. She had a lonely and unhappy childhood. Her father died when she was only a few months old. Her uncle, King William IV, had no children, and Victoria would inherit the throne when he died. So her mother kept a close watch on her. Victoria rarely went out.

The young princess met few other children. Her only friend was her stern German governess, Baroness Lehzen. Victoria grew up to be stubborn and quick-tempered, but also dignified and truthful. When told she would be the next monarch, she replied, "I will be good".

▽ **A painting of the young Victoria in 1830.** As a teenager, she was plain and dumpy. But she was taught to move gracefully. She even had a sprig of holly tied under her chin to make her hold up her head. The princess loved parties, but was seldom allowed to meet boys of her own age.

△ **Kensington Palace and its gardens in London**, where Victoria was born in 1819. Although it was a grand house, the furniture was plain and the carpets worn. Meals were dull, and a cup of tea was 'a great treat'. Victoria disliked palaces for the rest of her life.

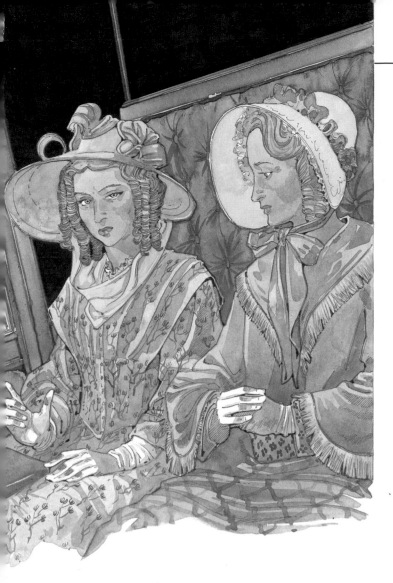

Between 1832 and 1835, Victoria was sent on a series of coach journeys through Britain. Her mother believed that she should see the country she would one day be ruling. The princess travelled to North Wales, the Midlands, Yorkshire, the south coast and East Anglia. She stayed in hotels, or grand houses such as Chatsworth and Alton Towers (then a private house). Wherever she went, she was greeted with banners, speeches and concerts in her honour. She described what she saw in a diary.

It was her first sight of the way poor people lived in Britain. She did not know that thousands of children, some as young as seven, had to work in mills and factories instead of going to school. Their jobs were in factories, down mines, or out in the city streets. The employers preferred child workers because they could pay them less than adults. A child might earn £10 (£500 at today's value) a year. When she became queen, Victoria was paid £385,000 a year.

△ **Princess Victoria on her journey through the Midlands in 1832.** This was not a holiday, but part of her education. She had already been taught many subjects, including:
- history
- geography
- Latin
- French
- religion
- poetry
- handwriting
- drawing
- the piano
- singing
- dancing.

△ **A chimney sweep.** Small boys were sent up narrow chimneys to clean them. Some chimneys were still hot.

△ **Young children worked in coal mines** for hours in the dark. They opened and shut traps to let wagons through.

△ **A factory worker.** Some children in cotton mills such as this worked for 16 hours a day among dangerous machines.

FACTORIES AND TOWNS

Towns were growing rapidly. In 1801, the first census showed that only about one-third of the British population lived in towns. By 1851, this had gone up to a half. Ten cities, including Manchester, Liverpool and Glasgow, had more than 100,000 inhabitants. Biggest of all was London, with nearly 2,500,000.

△ **A 'truck' token.** Some workers were paid with these coins, which could only be spent at the shop run by the company.

People flocked from the countryside to the towns. They came to find work and earn more money. The wages of a farm worker were very low, and there were fewer jobs on the land, thanks mainly to new machines such as threshers. But thousands of new workers were needed to operate machines in mills and foundries. Factory owners built houses for them.

The workers' houses were usually near the factories, so that people could walk to work. They were built as quickly and cheaply as possible. Most houses in the North of England were 'back-to-backs', built in double rows. In Scotland, many workers lived in blocks of flats called tenements. The houses were crammed close together, with narrow streets between. Chimneys, bridges and factory smoke blocked out much of the light.

Almost all these houses were crowded. Five or more people might live in a small single room. Even the cellars were full. In Liverpool in the 1840s, there were 4,400 cellars and nearly 40,000 people living in them.

Most of the new towns were also very dirty and unhealthy. The household rubbish was simply thrown out into the streets. In Manchester in 1832, nearly half of the streets were unpaved and covered in filth, including dung and rotten food. They were an ideal place for germs to breed. More than 31,000 people died during an outbreak of the cholera in 1832, and many more were killed by typhus, smallpox and dysentery.

△ **Poor people selling second-hand goods** in the streets of Houndsditch, London, in 1872. One stall has bottles, a violin and saw. Another has old clothes.

◁▽ **A view of an industrial town in the late 1830s.** The houses and factory buildings are crammed close together. The chimneys of the metal works belch out the smoke from furnaces, filling the air with dust and soot. At the bottom left is the canal which runs beside the works. Boats bring coal and iron from the nearest mines. They also carry the finished goods from the factory all over the country.

▷ **A cartoon** showing a rich man ignoring the poor.

THE POWER OF STEAM

Many more uses were found for steam power during the early 19th century. The engines built by James Watt in the 1770s had been used to pump water from mines and work machines in factories. Now, inventors developed steam engines which could move themselves. The railway age had begun.

The first public railway linked the coal mines of Darlington with the port of Stockton. It was built by engineer George Stephenson and opened in 1825. Five years later, he completed another line between Liverpool and Manchester. It was a huge success. By 1835 it was carrying 156,000 tonnes of goods and 470,000 passengers a year.

Railways were not just faster and stronger than other kinds of transport. They were cheaper too. The cost of train travel was about half that of a stage coach. And, for the first time, people could travel more swiftly than a galloping horse. The railways carried food, supplies and people to the growing factory towns.

More lines were quickly built. In 1841 the Great Western Railway, designed by Isambard Kingdom Brunel, joined London to Bristol. By 1855 there were over 13,000 kilometres of track in Britain.

Many people hated the railways. Farmers and landowners feared that their property would be damaged as new track was laid. Coach and canal owners saw that the railways would put them out of business. Ordinary people were frightened of the speed and the flying sparks from the huge locomotives.

▷ **A Great Western train** comes out of Box Tunnel in Wiltshire. This tunnel was 3 kilometres long (the longest in the world at the time) and took 5 years to dig. Almost all the work of building the railways was done by hand. Armies of men, using only picks, shovels and barrows, made cuttings and tunnels. These men were called navigators, or navvies for short. Many were from Ireland, where there were few jobs.

▽ **The Railway Station** – a Victorian painting.

△ **Isambard Kingdom Brunel**, one of the greatest Victorian engineers. He built steam ships, such as the *Great Western* (shown left), and bridges, as well as railways.

▽ **The railway network in the early 1850s.** Between 1844 and 1848 there had been a rush to build new lines. This was called 'railway mania'. By 1852 all the main routes in Britain had been built.

Victoria Becomes Queen

"Poor little Queen! She is at an age at which a girl can hardly be trusted to choose a bonnet for herself; yet a task is laid upon her from which an archangel might shrink." Thomas Carlyle wrote this after Victoria's coronation in 1838. When she had come to the throne, the queen was only 18 years old.

King William IV, Victoria's uncle, died on 20 June 1837. Early that morning, the princess was woken up and told that she was Britain's new ruler. At 11 o'clock, she had her first meeting with her Privy Councillors (chief ministers). She impressed them all with her calmness.

Victoria's closest advisor and friend during the early years of her reign was the Prime Minister, Lord Melbourne. He taught the queen much about politics and government. At the time there were two political parties, the Tories and the Whigs. Melbourne was a Whig.

In 1839, Victoria was visited by her cousin Albert, a German prince. Her family thought that he would make an ideal husband for her, and the queen soon fell in love. The couple were married in February 1840 in London.

At first, many people distrusted the prince because he was a foreigner. But Albert soon became respected for his hard work and his interest in science, the arts and education. He helped reform the army, and encouraged the building of new museums, including the Natural History Museum in London. The marriage made Victoria very happy. Albert was not just her husband, but also her private secretary.

▷ **Stamp and coins** from Victoria's reign. The Penny Black of 1840 and Penny Red of 1841 were the world's first sticky stamps.

That summer, while the queen was riding in an open carriage from Buckingham Palace, a gunman shot at her twice. She was unharmed, but this was only the first of seven attempts to kill her during her reign. (They all failed.) Victoria showed great courage, and when she next went out to the opera, she was cheered wildly by a large crowd.

The greatest tragedy of Victoria's life struck in 1861, when Albert died of typhoid fever. After this, she seldom went out in public. She wore black mourning clothes and spent much time at remote Balmoral Castle in Scotland.

◁ **The new queen attends her first Privy Council meeting** in Kensington Palace in 1837. This painting shows Lord Melbourne (seated, holding the pen), the Prime Minister, with Lord Palmerston (seated behind him), the Duke of Wellington (standing before the pillar), and Sir Robert Peel (on his left). (Both Palmerston and Peel became Prime Minister later in her reign.) Victoria read out a speech written for her by Lord Melbourne.

△ **Victoria and Prince Albert** after their wedding at St James's Palace. Albert disliked banquets and life in London. He encouraged the queen to spend more time at Windsor Castle and the Isle of Wight.

▷ **A painting by the queen** of Prince Alfred and Princess Alice. Between 1840 and 1857, Victoria had four sons and five daughters. The eldest, Albert Edward, became King Edward VII.

THE GROWTH OF TRADE

Victoria's reign saw the start of 'free trade' for British farmers and manufacturers. Since Stuart times, Parliament had tried to protect British agriculture and industry from foreign rivals. It had set duties (extra payments) on many goods imported from abroad and had passed Corn Laws to control the import of grain.

Many people believed that this protection harmed British trade, and kept the price of corn too high. An Anti-Corn Law League was formed. In 1846 the Corn Laws were repealed (abolished) by the Conservative Prime Minister Robert Peel. By 1852, duty had been taken away from most goods. Other European countries became 'free traders' too.

Britain swiftly grew to be the world's richest trading nation. Without duty, raw materials such as cotton could be imported more cheaply. At the same time, more factories, mills and foundries were built. Using new manufacturing processes and steam power, they made machines, textiles, ships and other goods that were sold overseas.

▽ **Sir Robert Peel** became Tory Prime Minister in 1841. Many Tory MPs were angry when he did away with the Corn Laws, and he was forced to resign. In 1829, Peel had created the first police force in London.

▽ **This chart shows how Britain's trade grew** between 1850 and 1870. More goods were imported than exported. But trades involving services such as banking, rather than goods, brought a great deal of money into the country.

	Imports	Exports	Service trades
1850s	169.5	100.1	101
1860s	260.9	159.7	187
1870s	360.6	218.1	288

(Figures are a yearly average over each decade. They are in £millions.)

▷ **Building the Crystal Palace in London**, to house the Great Exhibition of 1851. It was designed by Joseph Paxton and made of iron and glass. The iron framework was lifted into place, a section at a time, by two huge cranes. The Palace was 563 metres long and 139 metres wide, and covered an area the size of four football pitches. It was an ideal home for sparrows, which were a nuisance. No-one could find a way to get rid of them, until the Duke of Wellington suggested sparrowhawks. This worked.

On 1 May 1851, the queen opened the Great Exhibition in the Crystal Palace in Hyde Park, London. It had been planned by Prince Albert to show off many of the marvellous products and inventions of the age. The huge building contained over 7,000 exhibits from Britain and 6,000 from overseas.

Crowds flocked in to stare at the wonders on show. Among them were steam locomotives, a steam hammer, delicate pottery and Swiss watches, an envelope-making machine and a cast-iron fountain. There was even a model of the docks at Liverpool, with 1,600 fully-rigged ships.

It proved that Britain was the 'workshop of the world'.

△ **The completed Crystal Palace.** It was built in less than 7 months due to the use of mass-produced parts of the same shape and size, steam-driven machines and a team of 2,260 men. The Exhibition was a huge success, with six million visitors in 140 days.

TROUBLES ABROAD

By 1850, there had been no major war in Europe for 35 years. During this period of peace, Britain's army, although small, had grown strong, and controlled a growing empire. Her navy ruled the ocean from the Atlantic to the China Seas. But in 1853 Turkey declared war on Russia. The Crimean War had begun.

▽ **A map of the Crimea**, an area which juts out from Russia into the Black Sea. The main battles of the war were:
● Alma – a costly victory for the allies
● Balaclava – a Russian attack was driven off
● Inkerman – another Russian attack failed
● Sebastopol – allied guns bombarded the town for 11 months.

RUSSIAN EMPIRE

CRIMEA

Sebastopol • Alma
Balaclava • Inkerman

BLACK SEA

△ **Florence Nightingale** went to the Crimea with 38 nurses to care for the wounded. At Scutari Hospital, she soon had 5,000 soldiers to look after, and was working 20 hours a day.

◁ **British soldiers in the Crimea.** Allied and Russian armies suffered badly from icy weather, outbreaks of disease as well as fierce fighting.

The war was fought between Russia and the allied armies of Britain, France, Turkey and Sardinia. The allies wanted to stop Russia from seizing territory ruled by Turkey. The allied army of 60,000 men landed in the Crimea in September 1854. It defeated the Russians at Alma and marched on to besiege Sebastopol. The war was to last for over a year.

In October, the Russians made a suprise attack on the British base at Balaclava. During the battle, the British 'Light Brigade' of cavalry charged the main Russian army by mistake. Out of 673 men, 247 were killed or wounded.

Winter came, and the allied soldiers had to live in terrible conditions. Few had shelter from the cold, or enough food or medicine. Thousands died from disease or wounds. Sebastopol fell at last in September 1855, and the Russians were forced to make peace in February 1856. Each side had suffered many casualties.

The Indian Mutiny broke out in 1857. These are some of the causes:
● Indians disliked the way that the British were trying to change their way of life.
● They feared that the British would force them to become Christians.
● All Indian soldiers had to promise that they would fight anywhere in the empire.
● New cartridges were issued to the Indian troops. The cartridges were covered with animal grease – either from pigs (which the Muslims thought unclean) or from cows (which the Hindus thought sacred).
● The setbacks of the Crimean War had shown the Indians that the British were not all-powerful.

▷ **British troops charge at Indian rebels** in Lucknow in March 1858. There were only 34,000 British soldiers in the Indian army, while there were more than 250,000 Indian troops.

▽ **Photograph of British supply ships** in the harbour at Balaclava.

Only a year later, the British faced an uprising in India. Three regiments of Indian soldiers mutinied in May 1857. They captured the city of Delhi. The mutiny quickly spread through central India, and hundreds of Europeans were killed. Cawnpore was captured, and rebels surrounded Lucknow. But the mutineers had no proper leader. By early 1858, British troops had driven them out of Delhi and other cities, and killed thousands in a terrible revenge.

CHURCH AND CHAPEL

"Pews for the rich were padded, lined and cushioned. The poor were seated on stools in the aisles…and the cold, damp stone beneath their feet was the only place to kneel in prayer." This description of an Ipswich church was written in 1850.

The writer is referring to a church which belonged to the Church of England, or Anglican religion. This was the established Christian faith in Britain. Queen Victoria was an Anglican, and so were most rich and middle class people. But few working people went to Anglican churches. They felt out of place, and disliked the hard seats. Worse still, they thought that most parsons were supporters of the landowners.
Other kinds of Christianity, such as Methodism and Baptism, had begun by attracting working people. Their services were simple, and held in plain chapels. But by the 1850s most chapel-goers were middle class. The working classes, especially those in the towns, seldom had time to go to church.

▽ **A Sunday service at an Anglican church**. The parson preaches his sermon from the pulpit. It might last for a whole hour. Most middle class families went to church at least once on Sundays. Some went two or three times. Sunday was thought to be 'the Lord's Day', and so no work was supposed to be done. Children had to stay at home and read religious books. For working people, Sunday was usually their only day of rest.

▷ **A cartoon of 1861 connected with Charles Darwin**'s theory of evolution. Darwin suggested that humans had evolved (changed gradually) from apes. Darwin's most famous book was *The Origin of Species* (1859). This said that the Earth was much older than most people thought, and that animals and plants had evolved over millions of years. Darwin's theory caused an uproar because it disagreed with the story of creation given in the Bible. Many Christians believed that everything in the Bible was true and should not be questioned.

MONKEYANA.

AM I A MAN AND A BROTHER?

▷ **The Earl of Shaftesbury** and his supporters at a community meeting. He believed it was his duty to God to help the poor. He entered Parliament in 1826, and in the 1830s and 1840s pushed through Parliament a series of Acts to improve the working conditions in factories and coal mines. Later he started 'ragged schools' for poor children and 'soup kitchens' where food was given free to the hungry.

△ **Chapels were a focus for social life**, as here at a Methodist chapel in Wales. So too were Methodist schools and public libraries.

In 1851, a census (survey) was made in England and Wales of people who went to church on Sundays. It showed that less than half of the population of about 18 million attended a religious service. And only about 5 million of these were members of the Church of England.

Church leaders were shocked, and tried to reform their faiths. One group of Anglicans, the Evangelicals, realized that the Church should do more to help the poor in the towns. They set up many charities and social clubs in London and industrial cities. Men such as Lord Shaftesbury led campaigns to improve the conditions for people who worked in mines and factories.

The Evangelicals grew into the strongest religious force in Victorian Britain. They believed that all people were sinners, and could only be saved from hell by being sorry for their sins and leading a strict moral life. They held family prayers in their homes. Their missionaries went to Africa and the East to convert people to their faith.

IN THE SUBURBS

By the 1860s, many industrial towns were overcrowded. The centres were clogged with shops, factories and busy streets. London alone contained nearly three million people. The only space for new housing lay in the countryside outside the towns.

The edges of towns were called the suburbs. At first, only the wealthy could afford to live so far from their workplaces. But public transport soon became cheaper and quicker. Regular horse-drawn bus services had begun in the 1830s. In 1863 the first London Underground railway opened. Electric trams started running in big cities such as Leeds and Birmingham in the 1890s.

Now many people were able to move to the suburbs and 'commute' to work each day. Huge areas of new housing were built. There was room for the houses to be larger than in the centres, with big gardens and wide roads between. Most were set together in terraces, though more expensive houses were separate, or 'detached'.

△ **Three blocks of flats built in Islington, London, in 1879.** These were called New Model Dwellings, and were built to provide healthy and comfortable homes for working people. About 2,000 people lived in them. They paid a rent of just over 2 shillings (equivalent to about £5 at today's value) each week.

◁ **A baby's bath**, towels and can for carrying water. Very few houses had bathrooms or lavatories. Even Buckingham Palace had none when Victoria began her reign. Most people used outside lavatories, called 'privies'. It was not until the end of the century that houses were supplied with running water from the mains.

▽ **A large suburban house in the 1880s.** It stands on the end of a terrace and has a glass conservatory. The house is built of red and grey bricks, with moulded bricks around the windows. The rooms are lit by gas and heated by coal fires. The coal is stored in a cellar under the house.

◁ **The street** is busy with tradesmen delivering goods to the houses. Letters are collected regularly from the pillar box, introduced in 1855.

25

EXPLORERS AND MISSIONARIES

Many Victorian travellers set out for little-known parts of the world. Some went to trade, some to secure new territory for the British Empire. Missionaries, like David Livingstone, went to convert people to the Christian faith. But others went simply to explore, and to solve age-old mysteries.

Many of these mysteries lay in Africa, then known as 'The Dark Continent'. In 1857, John Hanning Speke set out to explore the great lakes of equatorial Africa. After several years he showed that the mighty River Nile flowed out of a huge lake (which he named Lake Victoria). Other famous travellers came to the river. In 1864, Samuel Baker found a smaller lake further down the Nile (Lake Albert). And in 1875, Henry Morton Stanley sailed round Lake Victoria to prove that Speke had been right.

▽ **Victorian travellers in Africa took a mountain of equipment.** Here are some of the articles carried by porters on the expeditions of Speke, Baker and Stanley:

● rifles and pistols for hunting or protection from attack
● beads, silk cloth, blankets, cutlery and watches for presents or for trading
● an enamel bath
● a Persian carpet
● a wooden boat, made into five sections, which could be put together for sailing on Lake Victoria
● an iron chair
● tinned food from Fortnum & Mason store in London
● tents and other camping equipment
● medicine chests.

▽ **Speke and his party of native carriers** on the way to Lake Victoria.

▽ **A large suburban house in the 1880s.** It stands on the end of a terrace and has a glass conservatory. The house is built of red and grey bricks, with moulded bricks around the windows. The rooms are lit by gas and heated by coal fires. The coal is stored in a cellar under the house.

◁ **The street** is busy with tradesmen delivering goods to the houses. Letters are collected regularly from the pillar box, introduced in 1855.

COUNTRY LIFE

During the 1850s there was a boom in farming. The new towns needed supplies of food. Grain and meat prices were high, and farmers could sell all they grew. But by 1875 the boom was over. Cheaper wheat began to flood in from the USA, and cheaper meat from Argentina and Australia. Food prices fell rapidly.

At the same time there was a series of bad harvests, and disease killed many cattle and sheep. Many farmers were ruined. But life was hardest for the farm labourers. There were now fewer jobs on the land than ever. New machines, such as steam threshers, saved time and needed few men to operate them.

△ **Victorian photograph of a ploughman** with his team of horses, taking a break from work. In 1850 the steam plough was invented, but it was not widely used for some years. It was hauled by steam engines.

△ **A squire with his family and servants** outside his country house at Ketteringham near Norwich in 1865. While the servants of town houses were often not essential to the running of a home but were luxuries, many people were needed to run country mansions and their vast estates. They included cooks, maids, gardeners and gamekeepers. Some great houses had over 100 servants.

▷ **Some of the main jobs on the farm in the 1880s:**

● Harvesting. The harvester (right) cut the corn with a sickle or scythe, which he kept very sharp. He could cut an area the size of a football pitch in a day.

● Haymaking. Women helped to turn the grass after it was mown (centre right) so that it would dry in the sun and wind. The hay was stored in tall stacks and fed to animals through the winter.

● Packing fruit and vegetables to take to market. (A market is shown far right.)

▽ **A steam-powered threshing machine at work.** The wheat was fed in and separated into grain and straw. Before this, threshing was done by hand. It was a long job which had earned the labourers much-needed extra money for winter.

The people who owned most of the land were very rich. A typical squire of the 1880s earned at least £3,000 a year from renting out land to farmers. But the people who worked on the land were very poor. Even in the 1880s, some farm labourers earned less than 10 shillings (50 pence) a week, with extra wages paid in beer, milk or firewood.

Many workers rented their cottages from the farmer. The cottages were often very small, with only two rooms, and dark, damp and draughty. If the worker lost his job, he would probably lose his home as well, and go to live in the parish workhouse. Some landowners looked after their labourers better. The Prince of Wales had over 70 new cottages built for his workers at Sandringham in Norfolk.

Many villagers kept a pig in their gardens, and grew vegetables. These were their chief source of food. Some got extra meat by poaching rabbits or pheasants from the squire's land. Any poacher who was caught would be fined or sent to prison.

After the slump of 1875, many workers moved to the towns, where they were better paid and worked shorter hours. In 1851, there were 1.3 million farmworkers. By 1901, there were only 0.7 million left.

EDUCATION

Until the 1840s, children did not have to go to school – and very few of them did. Even in 1861, a government report showed that of the population of 21 million there were only 2.5 million children at elementary (primary) schools. Many of these only went for less than a year, and few stayed on after the age of 10.

Education cost money. Wealthy people could afford to hire a governess or a tutor to teach their children at home. When they were older, the sons would be sent to stay (board) at a public school such as Eton or Rugby. The daughters were kept at home, and taught sewing, singing and playing the piano.

Poor people also had to pay to send their children to school. Schools cost parents at least a penny a week for each child, and few working class families could afford this. The parents also needed the money the children could earn by working.

△ **A young boy sells matches in the street.** He is so poor that he has no shoes. Thousands of children never went to school at all, but worked on the streets to earn extra money for their families. Some sold flowers and fruit, and some swept roads.

Improved education
During Victoria's reign, schools were made better in many ways:
1840 The first teacher training college opens at Battersea in London.
1846 Clever pupils are used as teachers; some are only 10 years old.

1870 Education Act gives power to local school boards to start schools.
1880 Every child has to go to school between the ages of 5 and 10.

1891 Elementary education becomes free for all children.
1899 The school leaving age is raised to 12. Art and science are taught.

△ **A child scaring birds** from a wheat field with a rattle. There were many odd jobs which kept country children away from school. Some worked in field gangs, gathering stones, pulling turnips or stacking corn. The wages were vital to their families.

△ **A child sells newspapers.** As more people learned to read, newspapers became much more popular. In 1890, Britain's first daily newspaper with pictures, the *Daily Graphic*, was published.

▷ **Illustrated page from Dickens'** *Oliver Twist* (far right) showing Fagin, the organizer of child crime, in prison.

△ **Charles Dickens** was the most famous writer of the age. His novels included *Nicholas Nickleby*, which attacked the cruelty and bad conditions at cheap public (boarding) schools, and *Oliver Twist*, a tale of child thieves and poverty in London.

◁ △ **Victorian classroom objects.** These included a handbell, Bible and pupil's spectacles (far left), desk, slate and slate pencil (left), and writing books and ink pen (above).

There were several kinds of school for poorer children. The youngest might go to a 'Dame' school, run by a local woman in a room of her house. The older ones went to a day school. There, the teacher was probably a local tradesman who made extra money by taking in pupils. Such schools were often dirty and very crowded.

Other schools were organized by churches and charities. Among these were the 'ragged' schools, which were first set up in 1844 for orphans and very poor children. Schools like this had to be run very cheaply. They had few books apart from Bibles. Most of the teaching was done by 'monitors' – older pupils who taught simple lessons to the younger ones.

School life was often very dull. Children were taught little apart from the 'three Rs' – Reading, 'Rriting and 'Rithmetic. They read aloud from books, which usually contained passages from the Bible. They wrote and did their sums usually using chalk on slates.

PASTIMES

By the second half of Victoria's reign, most people earned more money and worked shorter hours than ever before. For the first time, ordinary workers had enough leisure time to enjoy sports and other pastimes, and even to go away for holidays to the seaside.

△ **Cycling** became very popular. When the 'safety bicycle' appeared in 1885, it was the cheapest way to travel. Townsfolk used bicycles to ride out into the countryside.

△ **Children play** in the street with an iron hoop. Most working class children spent their playtime out of doors, playing football, chasing games or hopscotch.

▷ **Families pack into Terry's Theatre, London, in the 1880s** to watch a song-and-dance show. Places where people could go to be entertained included:
● **Theatres** Most large towns had several theatres.
● **Music halls** These were cheap and very popular.
● **Circuses** Circus companies toured the country.
● **Fairs** Most fairs took place on local holidays.

◁ **Entertainment, celebrations and enjoyment** on the beach at Ramsgate, Kent, in July 1887.

Games such as football and cricket had been played for centuries. Now they were organized and given strict rules. The first FA (Football Association) Cup Final was played in 1871. During the 1880s, many of today's Football League clubs were established.

English and Australian teams played the first cricket Test Match in England in 1880. Among the players was W.G. Grace, the greatest sportsman of the age.

These organized matches soon drew large crowds. Watching had now become a pastime. But growing numbers also took part in new sports like cycling, croquet, boating or lawn tennis. During the 1870s, roller skating became a craze.

Meanwhile many old, crueller sports slowly disappeared. Bull-baiting had been banned by law in 1835. By 1849, cock-fighting was illegal too. But hangings were still public events until as late as 1868, and were always popular.

In 1871, the Bank Holiday Act declared that certain days throughout the year were official holidays (when banks and offices closed). The speed of railway transport meant that people could spend their days off at the seaside. Coastal towns such as Blackpool, Southend, Morecambe and Brighton quickly grew into popular holiday resorts. In the cities, people could also enjoy the new parks, zoos and museums.

▽ **Reconstruction of a Victorian nursery.** Girls in wealthy families had expensive toys such as rocking horses or doll's houses. Boys played with metal miniature soldiers or clockwork models. Poorer children bought their toys at penny bazaars. For one penny they could buy pencils, beads, tiny dolls or tin badges.

WORKSHOP OF THE WORLD

British industry reached its peak in about 1890. In 1892, three out of every four new ships in the world were built in Britain. Cotton textiles, steel, machines, minerals and coal were being sold as far away as Australia, India and Canada.

The main raw materials for this success were coal and iron. New mining methods meant that more coal could be cut, and production shot up from 50 million tonnes in 1850 to over 150 million tonnes in 1890. With Henry Bessemer's invention of his converter in 1856, steel could at last be made from iron quickly and cheaply.

Steel was stronger and less brittle than iron, and many new uses were found for it. Railways were re-laid with steel track. Great steel bridges were built to carry the lines over wide rivers and estuaries. The biggest of these was the Forth Bridge, which was completed in 1890.

Steel also brought a great change to shipbuilding. It was lighter than iron, so bigger ships could be made. These new boats had propellers, powered by steam engines. Steam power began to take over from sail. In 1900, there were nearly as many steam ships as sailing ships.

Many important new uses were being found for steam. By the 1880s, steam engines were turning dynamos to make electricity in power stations. The electricity was used to drive factory machines. Then, in 1882, Joseph Swan set up generating stations. Soon, electric street lighting was introduced. Even some lighthouses had electric lights.

△ **Trial run on London's first Underground Railway** in 1863 between Paddington and the City.

▽ **An engineer's drawing** of 1880 for new street subways for sewers and pipes leading to shops and offices.

△ **Advert for a new type of dye** for sale in America, from about 1880.

Important advances in British industry:
1845 Alexander Parkes makes the first plastic from wood fibres.
1856 William Perkin makes a purple dye (aniline) from coal tar – the first artificial dye. Henry Bessemer invents the steel-converter.
1867 William Siemens invents an even more efficient 'open-hearth' method of steelmaking.
1885 The railway tunnel is completed beneath the River Severn.
1890 Electric trains run on the London Underground. A power station first supplies electricity to the City.
1893 Ship Canal links Manchester docks with the sea.

◁ **A busy sea port** at the height of Britain's industrial age. Trains carry goods and passengers across a steel bridge. Steamships have been loaded with cargo bound for customers overseas.

THE IRISH PROBLEM

By the 1840s, there were over eight million people in Ireland. At least half of them were poor peasants who rented tiny farms from landowners. Their main source of food was the potatoes they grew in their fields. But in 1845 this vital crop was destroyed by a disease called blight. In 1846, it struck Ireland again.

▷ **Policemen, bailiffs and English soldiers** get ready to evict an Irish peasant farmer in 1850. Most peasants lived in huts like this, made of stones, sticks and turf. The failure of the potato crop, and bad harvests of oats and barley, left the farmers with too little money to pay their rents. Between 1849 and 1852, more than 58,000 people were evicted and left homeless because they were behind on their rents. Some peasants fought back by burning ricks and threatening landowners.

The famine which followed was a calamity for Irish peasants. Nearly a million people died. Thousands more fled the country to find better conditions abroad. Between 1840 and 1860, two million Irish people emigrated to America. The British government was slow to give help. Worse still, it gave no protection to peasant farmers who were too poor to pay the rents on their land. Many were evicted (thrown out) from their homes by the landowners, most of whom lived in England.

The demand for Irish Home Rule grew stronger. In 1859, a secret society called the Fenian Brotherhood was formed. Its aim was to make Ireland independent, by force if necessary. They tried to seize Chester Castle in 1867, but were driven off. They also blew up a London prison, killing 12 people.

▷ **Irish emigrants wait at Liverpool docks** to board their ship to North America. Between 1800 and 1875, over 7.5 million people took this route. More than half of them were Irish. The early emigrant ships were powered by sail, and took seven weeks to cross the Atlantic. Poorer passengers were crammed together in the 'steerage', below decks in the stern.

◁ **A cartoon of 1870 showing Gladstone** struggling with the problem of English landlords in Ireland. Gladstone became Prime Minister for the third time in 1886, and tried to have a Home Rule Bill passed by Parliament. But many in Gladstone's party (the Liberals) were against the Bill, and it was rejected. Gladstone's second Home Rule Bill of 1893 was defeated in the House of Lords.

△ **Charles Stewart Parnell** was a Protestant who became leader of the Irish Home Rule Party in 1877.

Unrest continued to grow in Ireland. Bands of men called 'Moonlighters' attacked anyone who supported the English. A Home Rule Party was formed in 1870, and soon had 50 MPs. When Charles Stewart Parnell became its leader, he tried to get attention for its cause.

But the violence went on. In 1882, Irish terrorists murdered Lord Cavendish and his under-secretary in Phoenix Park, Dublin. Disgust at this turned many people against Home Rule. All the same, the Irish gained more seats in Parliament. The Prime Minister, William Gladstone, now supported the idea of Home Rule. But his first attempt to give Ireland its independence failed, and he was voted out of office. Then in 1890, Parnell was involved in a scandal over his affair with a married woman. The Home Rule Party dismissed him as leader.

Without Parnell, the party had no real voice in Parliament. When Gladstone tried a second Home Rule Bill, it was thrown out by the House of Lords. The Irish problem was far from being solved.

EXPLORERS AND MISSIONARIES

Many Victorian travellers set out for little-known parts of the world. Some went to trade, some to secure new territory for the British Empire. Missionaries, like David Livingstone, went to convert people to the Christian faith. But others went simply to explore, and to solve age-old mysteries.

Many of these mysteries lay in Africa, then known as 'The Dark Continent'. In 1857, John Hanning Speke set out to explore the great lakes of equatorial Africa. After several years he showed that the mighty River Nile flowed out of a huge lake (which he named Lake Victoria). Other famous travellers came to the river. In 1864, Samuel Baker found a smaller lake further down the Nile (Lake Albert). And in 1875, Henry Morton Stanley sailed round Lake Victoria to prove that Speke had been right.

▽ Victorian travellers in Africa took a mountain of equipment. Here are some of the articles carried by porters on the expeditions of Speke, Baker and Stanley:
● rifles and pistols for hunting or protection from attack
● beads, silk cloth, blankets, cutlery and watches for presents or for trading
● an enamel bath
● a Persian carpet
● a wooden boat, made into five sections, which could be put together for sailing on Lake Victoria
● an iron chair
● tinned food from Fortnum & Mason store in London
● tents and other camping equipment
● medicine chests.

▽ **Speke and his party of native carriers** on the way to Lake Victoria.

British explorers and where they went:
1848 Alfred Wallace and Henry Bates travel up the Amazon to Manaus.
1853 Richard Burton is the first white person to enter Mecca (in disguise).
1856 David Livingstone crosses Africa.
1860 Speke and Grant explore Lake Victoria.
1862 William Palgrave crosses Arabia.

1864 Samuel and Florence Baker reach Lake Albert in Africa.
1865 Edward Whymper climbs the highest peaks in the Andes.
1877 Stanley travels down the River Congo.
1891 Francis Younghusband crosses the Gobi Desert.
1893 Mary Kingsley travels in Angola and up the River Congo.

△ **Mary Kingsley** spent only a week in West Africa in 1897 but as a result she tried to change incorrect Victorian ideas about how Africans lived – they might not need 'civilising'.

△ **Sir John Franklin** made several voyages to the Arctic. In 1845 he set out to find a sea passage north of America. His ships *Erebus* and *Terror* were caught in the ice, and the entire party perished.

Another mystery was the North-West Passage. For two centuries, sailors had tried to find a northerly route from the Atlantic to the Pacific. Franklin's expedition of 1845 disappeared into the icy wastes. No fewer than 40 rescue parties were sent from Britain to search for them, but it was not until 1857 that the bodies were found.

△ **Henry Stanley greets Livingstone at Ujiji, East Africa, in 1871.** People in Britain thought Livingstone was dead, and Stanley was sent out to find him.

Far to the south, two British travellers were exploring the River Amazon in South America. Henry Bates and Alfred Wallace were naturalists. In 1848, they took boats up the river, collecting specimens of the animals and plants.

An even more amazing journey was made by Sir Richard Burton in 1853. Disguised in Arab clothes, he became the first 'white man' to enter the holy Muslim city of Mecca in Arabia.

THE BRITISH EMPIRE

"We hold a vaster empire than has been." These are the words on a Canadian stamp of 1898, showing a map of the British Empire. At its height, the empire covered one-fifth of the Earth's land surface, and contained over 370 million people.

Until about 1870, the empire had grown slowly. The British had gradually gained control of over half of India. Far Eastern ports in Singapore and Hong Kong had become important trading stations. Millions of settlers had emigrated to the wide open spaces of Canada, Australia, New Zealand and South Africa.

The only way to reach the eastern part of the empire was by sea, around the southern tip of Africa. In 1869, the new Suez Canal opened a direct link between the Mediterranean Sea and the Indian Ocean. This made the voyage between India and Britain much quicker. In 1875, Benjamin Disraeli (then Prime Minister) bought enough shares in the canal to give Britain control of it. This increased British power in the East. During the 1880s, parts of Borneo, Burma and New Guinea were added to the Empire.

Many men and much money were needed to control the growing British Empire. In 1893 the Army consisted of:
- 136,000 troops in Britain and Ireland
- 77,000 troops in India, supported by 160,000 Indian soldiers
- 47,000 troops in other territories, mainly South Africa and Egypt.

The Royal Navy had:
- 76,000 men
- 35 battleships
- 158 other warships.

▷ **The British Empire at its largest, in 1899.** The areas coloured red were under British control. They range from huge territories such as India, Canada and Australia to important islands such as Hong Kong, Singapore, Jamaica, and Ceylon in the Indian Ocean.

Canada
Bahamas
Jamaica
Sierra Leone
British Guiana
Gold Coast
Nigeria
Gambia
Aden
British East Africa
Ceylon
India
Burma
Hong Kong
British New Guinea
Singapore
South Africa
Australia
New Zealand

▷ **Singapore Harbour in the 1890s.** British residents take tea on deck. In the background is a Royal Naval gunboat, a symbol of British power. The island of Singapore was a major naval port, and a vital trading centre in South-East Asia. Rubber and other goods were shipped through here.

◁ **General Charles Gordon** at the fall of Khartoum in 1883. He was killed by followers of the Mahdi, leader of a Muslim revolt.

By 1880 only one continent remained to be colonized: Africa. Here, Britain had to compete with other empire builders, especially France and Belgium. Each country grabbed land in what was called the 'scramble for Africa'. Within a few years, Britain took control of large parts of Africa, including Kenya, Uganda, Nigeria and Egypt. British soldiers had to fight to hold on to these new territories. The bloodiest war took place in the Sudan in 1883, when rebels wiped out the British garrison at Khartoum.

▽ **Photograph of a tea plantation in India**, taken in 1876. British plantation managers oversee the work of local people.

END OF AN ERA

"To many of her people she is a name rather than a living reality." These were the words of *The Times* newspaper in 1887, when Victoria had been queen for 50 years. Since Albert's death in 1862 she had stayed in her palaces, and had rarely been seen by the public.

▷ **British troops wait for action during the Boer War.** The Boers were Dutch settlers in South Africa. In 1899 they rebelled against British rule. At first they had great success, defeating British armies three times during 'Black Week'. But the British slowly wore down Boer resistance, and they were forced to make peace in June 1902.

The queen at last emerged in June 1887 to celebrate her Golden Jubilee. She was taken through London to a thanksgiving service in Westminster Abbey. Cheering crowds lined the streets.

But the last years of the century were not all so happy. Britain was no longer the most important industrial nation in the world. She was challenged by the growing industrial power of the USA and Germany. Violence in Ireland was increasing. And one-third of Londoners lived in great poverty.

There were also troubles overseas. It was costly and difficult to keep control of the massive empire. During Victoria's reign, 230 wars had been fought. Most had been small, but the 1890s saw major conflicts with the Boers and Afghans.

◁ **Queen Victoria with relatives from all over Europe.** The photograph, taken just a few years before Victoria died, includes Edward Albert, William II of Germany and Czar Nicholas II of Russia. Edward Albert (known as 'Bertie') lived a very different kind of life from his strict and dignified mother. He enjoyed horseracing, gambling, sailing and huge banquets. He bought an estate at Sandringham in Norfolk, where he shot many pheasants. The queen thought he was lazy, and would not allow him to do any important work. By the time she died in 1901, Edward was 59 years old.

◁ **A family watches** from an upstairs window as the queen passes by in her coach during her Diamond Jubilee in 1897. Some people paid over £2 for a good view of the procession.

Despite the troubles, there were even greater celebrations at Victoria's Diamond Jubilee in June 1897. Once again she rode through London. To escort her, there were 50,000 troops from all parts of the empire. Among them were Australian cavalrymen, camel riders from Africa, head-hunters from Borneo and Indian princes. Royal Navy ships gathered at Spithead near Portsmouth on the south coast.

But by now the queen was an old woman. At the beginning of 1901 she was very weak. She died, aged 81, on 22 January. Her funeral was yet another grand state procession, but this time it marked the end of an era of British history. Victoria was buried beside Prince Albert at Windsor Castle.

Glossary

alliance an agreement to work or fight together.

anaesthetic a drug which puts patients to sleep or numbs an area of the body before an operation.

back-to-back houses two rows of houses built facing away from each other, so that their backs are joined.

ballot the total of votes in an election.

census official count and record of the population.

colony land in which people from a foreign country settle and that is ruled from a distance by that country.

commuting living in a suburb, or out of town, and travelling into the town to work each day.

coronation the ceremony of crowning a king or queen.

evolution the gradual change of something into a different form. Many Christians in Victorian times believed that animals could not evolve, but were exactly as they had been made by God.

flogging a punishment in which the wrongdoer is whipped or beaten.

foundry a factory where metal ore is melted down, purified and moulded.

governess a woman employed to teach and train children in a family.

government the people who run the country: the monarch, the Privy Council, Parliament and local officials.

Home Rule the freedom of a country to govern itself. This was the aim of Irish nationalists in the 1870s.

household people who work for or live with the owner of the house.

Liberals one of the two main parties in Parliament. It grew out of the Whig party of the early 19th century, and encouraged reform and free trade.

missionary a person who goes to do charitable or religious work in a foreign country.

music hall a show consisting of short acts, such as singing, dancing, conjuring and comedy.

mutiny an uprising against the people in command. It is usually used to describe rebellions in the army and navy.

Parliament the House of Lords (nobles and important churchmen) and the House of Commons (elected members) meeting to advise the monarch.

safety bicycle a bicycle with two wheel of the same size, driven by a chain. It was much safer than the old 'Penny Farthing', which had one big and one small wheel. (A farthing was a small Victorian coin, value ¼ of an old penny)

sewer an underground drain for carrying away dirty water.

slum an area of crowded and squalid housing.

suburb an area of housing built on the edge of a town.

tenement a large building divided into separate flats for rent.

textiles goods made from woven cloth.

Tory one of the two main parties in Parliament, which was to become the Conservative party. Most Tories opposed reform and supported the expansion of the empire.

tram a type of bus which ran on rails and was powered by electricity.

transportation punishment for a crime in which the prisoner was sent to work in a distant country, such as Australia.

turbine a machine containing a series of blades or buckets which are turned by the force of steam or water. Turbines are used to power engines or generate electricity.

vaccination the injection of a person with a mild form of a disease. This builds up protection against that disease.

Whigs the political party in Parliament which opposed the power of the monarch. It became better known as the Liberal party after the 1830s.

PLACES TO VISIT

Here are some museums and sites of Victorian interest to visit. Your local Tourist Office will be able to tell you about places in your area.

The Argory, County Tyrone, Northern Ireland Victorian house with a fascinating collection of furniture.

Biddulph Grange, Stoke-on-Trent Rare example of a Victorian garden, now being restored.

Bluebell Line, Horsted Keynes A working railway, with many steam locomotives.

Buckingham Palace, London Queen Victoria was the first to modernize this famous residence.

Calke Abbey, Derby Scarcely changed since the last century, it is full of day-to-day Victorian things.

Carlow County Museum, Carlow, Eire Nineteenth-century Irish exhibits.

Castle Museum, York Includes a reconstruction of a Victorian parlour.

Fox Talbot Museum, Lacock, Wiltshire A museum of photography, in memory of W.H. Fox Talbot, who lived here.

Gondola Steam Yacht, Coniston Water, Cumbria First launched in 1859, it still carries sightseers.

Great Britain, **Bristol Docks** Brunel's great iron ship, now being restored.

Hardy's Cottage, Bockhampton, Dorset Birthplace of the great poet and novelist Thomas Hardy.

Highland Folk Museum, Kingussie, Scotland Includes a copy of a turf-roofed hut lived in by 19th-century Scots.

Hughenden Manor, High Wycombe The home of Disraeli for over 30 years.

Knightshayes Court, Tiverton, Devon House with a richly decorated Victorian interior.

Museum of Childhood, Edinburgh Many Victorian toys and games.

Museum of English Rural Life, Reading Many photographs and tools of the Victorian countryside.

National Maritime Museum, Greenwich. The magnificent sailing ship *Cutty Sark* is moored here.

National Railway Museum, York A massive collection of old steam railway engines and rolling stock.

Natural History Museum, London One of the great and grand museums planned by Prince Albert. There are also many memorials to Albert in London.

North of England Open Air Museum, Beamish, County Durham Among the many reconstructions are a Victorian school room and miner's cottage.

Port Sunlight, Merseyside High-quality houses built for factory workers in the 1880s.

Royal Museum of Scotland The main hall is based on the design for the Crystal Palace.

St Gastayn Church, Llangasty, Powys A church in the 'Gothic Revival' style, fashionable in the early 1800s.

St Pancras Station, London A wonderfully grand building.

Welsh Industrial and Maritime Museum, Cardiff Many relics of the industrial revolution.

Windsor Castle, Berkshire Victoria and Albert are buried in the park.

INDEX